TATTOO ART FOR NEWBIES: Mastering the Basics

Yvette Sally

Table of Contents

CHAPTER ONE

INTRODUCTION

Is it substantial or not that you are a tattoo talented specialist searching for motivation? On the other hand maybe on a pursuit after ways to deal with refining your style and arrangement better tattoos and foster a more stylish portfolio. Then, at that point, you are flawlessly arranged. We'll detach the wanderer bits of tattoo plan. We'll let you know how to plan a tattoo that your clients will cherish and how to simultaneously make your own excellent style.

STRIKING TATTOO PLAN STYLES

Realness

Realness is one of the boldest furthermore one of the most prominent tattoo styles. It takes a ton of commitment to figure out a smart method for planning a tattoo in this style.

Photorealistic plans are tasteful and offer a remarkable explanation yet these are not the most straightforward to make. Since a ton goes into making the right shapes as features, shadows, and more to make importance and make your specialty look more logical.

Mathematical

Mathematical style is one that utilizes obviously depicted shapes and lines. There's a trademark ease in these tattoos that gets the news out. Precisely when you figure out a smart method for planning a tattoo consolidating mathematical shapes, you are learning a style that endures for an extremely huge stretch.

Tip: Mathematical tattoos look phenomenal both in faint and in arrangement. In any case, a ton relies on the shape you pick. To guarantee that your plan conveys the right opinions, figure out shape frontal cortex research while organizing a mathematical tattoo.

Quirk

Right when common shapes and plans are sufficient not, your response lies in idiosyncrasy. Particular tattoos combine two or three contemplations and reestablish them. These are explanation creators that can be adjusted in different ways.

The parts you join together and how you get them all help along with recapping various stories and there can also be different ways to deal with interpreting these plans. That is the thing makes them generally more surprising.

Control

For juveniles figuring out a viable method for planning a tattoo moderate styles are possible the most un-mentioning. There are decently several subtleties and layers in the tattoo. You don't need to stress over shadows and contorts to make a three-layered plan. Most moderate tattoos are level style and contain clear wreck free plans including by and large of clean lines.

Innate styles

Inherited tattoos are apparently the most enchanting styles concerning tattoo plan.

New school

This is perhaps of the latest style and is known for its particular energetic plans.

Unimportance is one of the remarkable bits of new school plans and they besides contain a great deal of eye-getting enthusiasm like subtleties. New school tattoos comparably have thick diagrams wanted to keep the picked marvelous groupings inside limits.

Black work

These are fast differences of new school styles since they just hold down faint lines and theoretical shapes. There are point by point designs and fascinating shapes utilized at any rate these don't utilize reasonable parts and particularly diserse plans. One of the prominent attributes of this style is the use of weak dull layouts and faint filled shapes changed by appalling spaces that assistance with making importance in the course of action. Right when you know your choices regarding the center style of your tattoo you are almost there. Then, comes the genuine solicitation of how to plan a tattoo. Might we at any point see two or three prescribed techniques and tips to assist with working on your work.

CHAPTER TWO

METHODOLOGY TO PLAN A TATTOO

As we examined over, the hidden step is picking your style. Right when you have shortlisted your style, the going with advances will get you to your ideal tattoo plan.

1. Know the position

Without a doubt, you can make two or three nonexclusive plans that can go in different pieces of the body. Notwithstanding, the best strategy for tweaking a tattoo and make it look regularly synchronized with the client's skin is to pick a game plan thinking about the position.

Precisely when you know where the tattoo will be inked, you will find out about the area open. This grants you to see the size of your game plan. While massive tattoos offer a striking explanation, putting them faultlessly arranged impacts whether they look their part. Some inadmissible spot can make an enormous tattoo turn stuffed vertical. Understanding the position additionally assists you with understanding the shapes your tattoo will cover. Since the state of your tattoo couldn't be ensured to appear, apparently, to be indistinct on all designs. The proposing that your tattoo course of action conveys with everything considered may be lost when the game plan seems, by all accounts, to be overseen or wound thinking about where it shows up. Along these lines, assuming you are contemplating how to plan a tattoo that your client would end up being terribly captivated with, bound down the position where the tattoo shows up before you freeze the course of action.

2. It's OK to search for motivation

A piece of the time you have everything to you yet you don't have even the remotest sign how to write the plan down and sometime later in ink. On the other hand a part of the time you wind up checking out at an undeniable screen not knowing what to plan. Without a doubt, even the most experienced tattoo specialists go through these stages.

To beat these circumstances and to find heading in your tattoo configuration process, it is really astute to search for motivation.

You could make loads up for various tattoo styles so that when your next tattoo project comes up, you can save the time spent chasing after the right motivation. You can additionally limit your choices in light of whether you are searching for Filipino ancestral styles or Polynesian, etc.

While it's OK to search for motivation, recollect that there's a dainty line between getting roused and duplicating a plan. You would need to make an extraordinary portfolio that exhibits your credibility. Clients love working with real tattoo specialists since that way they realize that they are getting a novel plan inked.

3. Each show-stopper starts as a sketch

At the point when you are sorting out some way to plan a tattoo don't pick convoluted plans. Most significant don't endeavor to make every one of the subtleties immediately. Separate your plan into segments and tackle them each in turn.

Sketch your thought on paper or utilize a computerized drawing tablet or even your iPad. Make sure to isolate the subtleties in your plan into various layers so you can make changes without returning to the entire plan.

From attracting the essential shapes to portraying over them generally and afterward adding the framework, filling tones, and adding subtleties and features each and every step can be isolated into layers when you draw your tattoo carefully. For pencil outlines utilize various sheets of following paper to put your layers one on top of the other.

4. Cautiously form your plan

When your plan is prepared, the last synthesis decides if you accomplish the expected impact or not. Tattoo plans are many times mixes of different shapes, bits of text, boundaries, complements, and different subtleties. In this way, the way this large number of components is joined can represent the moment of truth the impact. The piece of your plan incorporates everything from the extent of the components joined to their arrangement and positions. On account of computerized draws, you can continuously utilize a mockup to perceive how the tattoo looks on the genuine surface. This assists you with understanding whether the arrangement or position of explicit pieces of the plan should be changed. One more basic part of the structure of your tattoo configuration will be the differentiation. Indeed, even the most shocking plan won't have the expected effect assuming the difference is terrible. The underneath model shows how unfortunate differentiation ruins an incredible plan.

At long last, the most obvious boundary in your tattoo plans the varieties. When you conclude that it would be a shaded tattoo and not an all-dark plan, picking your variety range is a basic step. The tones impact the difference and subsequently the decipherability of the plan. On the off chance that you are working with monochrome ranges make sure to change the varieties in view of the client's complexion so the subtleties are flawless.

Tip: Varieties likewise have various temperaments and accordingly the general energy of the tattoo changes relying upon the tones utilized. Comprehend variety brain science and the significance of explicit variety mixes and variety ranges to explicit tattoo styles to accomplish the best outcomes. For instance, the specialty in the underneath tattoo configuration is the utilization of the right bit of varieties.

5. Remain educated regarding what's going on in the realm of tattoos

Knowing how to plan a tattoo isn't sufficient. You ought to likewise know how to convey your plans in the most proficient way. From clean practices to the utilization of the most recent inks and innovation, a great deal of differentiators put you aside in a cutthroat world. Assuming there are some new tattoo procedures that individuals are going wild over about, your clients can anticipate that you should convey them. Having the best plans won't do the trick in the event that you are not ready. For instance, Bang, a well known superstar tattoo craftsman as of late grown light-delicate inks. Lights of various frequencies help turn on and switch off various varieties in these tattoos. These are levels in personalization and such patterns are difficult to disregard. However, your plan ought to likewise be changed so that playing with various variety varieties and with various varieties being switched off won't let the message of the tattoo wander off. Invest energy refreshing yourself with all the most recent data in this industry so your plans continue to develop. That is one method for remaining ahead in the game.

CHAPTER THREE

ALTERNATE WAYS OF THINKING OF ONE OF A KIND TATTOO PLANS

Regardless of whether you know how to plan a tattoo, a new viewpoint generally makes a difference. In addition, you now and again essentially lack opportunity and energy to concoct new plans when your business keeps you occupied. All in all, what are your choices for making these extraordinary tattoo plans for your studio? Work with an independent planner, an artist to be explicit. Since you would need somebody who can think of cool ideas and characters and drawings without any preparation. Guarantee that your plan contract plainly discusses permitting and business utilization of the made plans. The way that you get limitless plans consistently makes it simpler to construct areas of strength for an in a brief time frame. Also, there are assorted sorts of plans shrouded in your membership. In this way, notwithstanding the custom tattoo plans for your business, you can likewise demand advertising plans to advance your tattoo studio without paying extra for something very similar. It's OK on the off chance that you don't expect customary plan work. Limitless plan memberships come without contracts. In this way, you can stop your membership whenever.

TATTOO PLAN PROCEDURES GUIDANCE FOR SPECIALISTS

As a fledgling tattoo craftsman, it very well may be difficult to go from a clear page to a total plan. In addition, it's much more testing to draw something that looks great on paper, however looks great on somebody's body.

Knowing the prescribed procedures while planning a tattoo won't just work on the nature of your work, however they will likewise make you more effective and decrease craftsman's block when you don't have the foggiest idea what to draw.

There are two distinct ways of planning a tattoo. You can all things considered:

• Draw it out on paper

• Plan it carefully

Note:

More often than not, you'll need to make a novel plan for every client. Notwithstanding, tattoo streak plans are straightforward tattoos that can be inked again and again. Whether you're drawing on paper or carefully, you'll in any case have to go through similar 3 stages.

1 Pick Reference Photographs

Finding great reference photographs will assist you with beginning conceptualizing as you set up your thoughts. They'll likewise give you something to begin with when you really begin drawing. Reference photographs are particularly significant for styles like authenticity.

2 Pick a Tattoo Style

What style you maintain that the tattoo should be will have a tremendous effect by the way you approach planning it. For instance, American conventional tattoos utilize thick strong lines and an exceptionally restricted variety range, while authenticity has no lines and can highlight any tones tracked down in a genuine photograph.

3 Pick a Variety Range

Which colors you decide to use in your tattoo configuration will to some extent rely upon the style you're planning in. Assuming your plan is in the American Conventional style, you'll need to stay with red, yellow, green, and dark. On the off chance that you're doing another everyday schedule piece, you can utilize splendid and strong tones. Furthermore, in the event that you're doing authenticity, your variety range will be directed by what your subject resembles, in actuality.

Note:

On the off chance that you're struggling with making a variety range, you can utilize Adobe Tone free of charge to produce and change custom ranges.

Plan Method 1: Hand-Drawing Your Tattoo Plan

We suggest attracting layers. This offers you a few chances to refine your work and become familiar with your plan prior to inking it.

Layer 1: Characterize essential shapes

Layer 2: Make your sketch

Layer: Areas of strength for 3 work

Layer 4: Add tone

Note:

Regardless of whether you're working with a tattoo style like American Customary that is renowned for explicit plans you can in any case make it your own by including your own subtleties and components. Every one of these layers can be various layers of following paper or white paper. This tries not to have any sketch lines on the last piece you'd show a client or put instantly sheet.

Plan Procedure 2: Advanced Tattoo Plan

In any event, while you're drawing carefully, working in layers is still best. Notwithstanding, you can simply import reference photographs as opposed to drawing them yourself. Every one of the components adjusted from photographs would be on an alternate "layer" in Photoshop or multiply, permitting them to cover. You can then utilize a stock picture of a body part to make a "model" of the tattoo to ensure it fits well on the body.

Ace Tip:

In the event that you're new to working carefully, take a stab at planning a dark and dim tattoo first. You'll have to delete everything in your reference photograph with the exception of the component you need to keep, desaturate it to turn it highly contrasting, knock up the differentiation, and afterward utilize the duplicate device to allow any white parts to appear as complexion.

Note:

Photoshop has a lofty expectation to learn and adapt. A full breakdown of how to involve Photoshop as a tattoo craftsman can be viewed as in the "Get Computerized" module of the Craftsman Gas pedal Program.

TATTOO CONFIGURATION RULES

Inking is a work of art, so there aren't many standards with regards to tattoo plans. Notwithstanding, on the off chance that you adhere to these rules, your tattoo plans will look much better on the body.

Incorporate a Closer view, Middleground, and Foundation

Heads Face In and Forward

Plans Need to Fit and Stream with the Body

Plan Methods to Consider:

Contrast: Complexion

Variety: Maturing

Line: Maturing (Section 2)

Negative Space: Skin Breaks

Detail: Situation

Understanding and utilizing plan methods is just the initial step to building an inking profession. Be that as it may, attempting to find all the data you want can be tedious and lead to inaccurate or even perilous propensities.

THE END